ABUNDANT TRUTH INTERNATIONAL MINISTRIES

Abundant Truth Spiritual Gifts Series

To Norma Lamb

A true woman of God. A woman of prayer, peace, and power.

The Promise of the Father

An Introduction to the Baptism of the Holy Spirit and the Gift of Tongues

Roderick Levi Evans

Published by Abundant Truth Publishing
P.O. Box 126
Camden, NC 27921
Web: www.abundantpublishing.net
Email: abundantpublishing@gmail.com
mailto:kbpublishing@live.com

Printed U.S.A.

Front & Back Cover Designs by Abundant Truth Publishing
All rights reserved.
Free-use Cover Image

Abundant Truth Publishing is a ministry of **Abundant Truth International Ministries.** The primary mission of ATI Ministries is to equip the Body of Christ with tools necessary to defend and contend for the truth of the Christian faith. Jesus Christ came to bear witness of the truth and ATI Ministries is a modern-day extension of His commission (John 18:37).

Abundant Truth Spiritual Gifts Series – The Promise of the Father
©2021 Abundant Truth Publishing
All Rights Reserved
ISBN13: 978-1601413086

Unless otherwise indicated, all of the scripture quotations are taken from the *Authorized King James Version* of the Bible. Scripture quotations marked with NIV are taken from the *New International Version* of the Bible. Scripture quotations marked with NASV are taken from the *New American Standard Version* of the Bible. Scripture quotations marked with Amplified are taken from the *Amplified Bi*

Printed in the United States of America

Contents

Introduction

1 – The Promise of the Father   1

The Ministry of the Holy Spirit   4

The Promise of the Father   12

The Foreshadowing of the Promise   16

2 – The Baptism of the Holy Spirit   37

Three Designations, One Event   41

The Promise Fulfilled   45

The Doctrine of the Baptism of the Holy Ghost   48

Contents (cont.)

3 – Physical Manifestations & the Baptism of the Holy Spirit — 59

Physical Manifestations in the Old Testament — 66

Physical Manifestations in the New Testament — 77

4 – The Gift of Tongues — 87

What is the Gift of Tongues? — 92

Prayer — 97

Prophecy — 99

Praise — 106

Interpretation of Tongues — 110

Contents *(cont.)*

5 – Questions & Answers **115**

Introduction

The promise of the Father was the fulfillment of God's prophecy through Joel. One result of the Spirit's coming would be prophetic revelation and the manifestation of dreams and visions. We discover from Paul's discussions of the gifts in I Corinthian 12 that the Spirit is responsible for the dispersion of the gifts. In the Abundant Truth Spiritual Gifts Series, we will examine the gifts of the Spirit and their operations in the New Testament Church.

In this publication:

In this book, we will discuss the fulfillment of Joe's prophecy at the Spirit's outpouring on Pentecost. Since that day, the ministry of the Holy Spirit is the prominent feature of the New Testament church. In the pages of this book, the dynamics of the promise of the Father; that is, the baptism of the Holy Spirit and the gift of tongues will be explored.

-1-
The Promise of the Father

THE PROMISE OF THE FATHER

THE PROMISE OF THE FATHER

In the beginning, God created the cosmos and all the elements contained therein. He spoke the word and by His power everything came into existence. The Book of Genesis reveals the agent of God's power, the Holy Spirit.

The Holy Spirit was given regard in the first verses of the scriptures along with God. This reveals the importance of His work in God's eternal purposes.

He is highlighted at the inauguration to demonstrate that He will always have a role in the affairs of men.

THE PROMISE OF THE FATHER

The Ministry of the Holy Spirit

After sin entered into the world, the Spirit of God was still "moving upon the faces of the deep" which resided in the hearts of men.

Hence, men were still aware of God and His righteous standards for His creation. Therefore, when God warns Noah of the coming judgment, He says that His Spirit will not always strive with men.

And the Lord said, My spirit shall not always strive with man, for that he also is flesh: yet his days shall be an

THE PROMISE OF THE FATHER

hundred and twenty years. (Genesis 6:3 KJV)

God did not say that "He" would not strive with men, but His Spirit's struggle will not continue with humankind. Jesus articulated what the "striving" of the Spirit consisted of.

And when he is come, he will reprove the world of sin, and of righteousness, and of judgment: (John 16:8 KJV)

The Holy Spirit was always present given men an inner conviction and awareness of sin and the existence of God. This is the primary work of the Spirit. Aside

THE PROMISE OF THE FATHER

from this, the Holy Spirt gave revelation, endowed men with power, and confirmed God's approval upon those whom He called.

Since all men were born sinners through the sin of Adam, there was need to bridge the gap in true fellowship and communion with God. This would be done by the working of the Holy Spirit in men's lives. Since the Holy Spirit was named at Creation, His role became to become a helper to the humans that were created.

After the mention of the Spirit of God in Genesis 6, the next time His working is

THE PROMISE OF THE FATHER

mentioned is by pharaoh concerning Joseph. After Joseph interpreted the dreams and offered him wise counsel as to what to do. Pharaoh commissions Joseph to oversee what needed to be done in response to the dream.

> *And the thing was good in the eyes of Pharaoh, and in the eyes of all his servants. And Pharaoh said unto his servants, Can we find such a one as this is, a man in whom the* **Spirit of God** *is? And Pharaoh said unto Joseph, Forasmuch as God hath shewed thee all this, there is none so*

THE PROMISE OF THE FATHER

discreet and wise as thou art: (Genesis 41:37–39 KJV Bold mine)

It is interesting to note that pharaoh used the same expressions that the Hebrews used to identify God. He proclaimed that the wisdom and revelation of Joseph came from the Spirit of God.

He used the same word for God that the Israelites used (Hebrew אֱלֹהִים[H430] elohiym). The term "elohim'" is used to describe God as the Supreme God.

Pharaoh asserted that the Spirit of the "Supreme" God resided in the man. From the biblical record, the progression of the

THE PROMISE OF THE FATHER

Holy Spirit's work is already seen from just outward miraculous works (i.e. creation) to operating in the life of His servants.

After His expressed identification in the events of Joseph's life, the expression "Spirit of God" is used by God to assure Moses of His choices of the head workman to construct the tabernacle.

*See, I have called by name Bezaleel the son of Uri, the son of Hur, of the tribe of Judah: And I have filled him with the **Spirit of God**, in wisdom, and in understanding, and in knowledge, and in all manner of workmanship, To*

THE PROMISE OF THE FATHER

devise cunning works, to work in gold, and in silver, and in brass. (Exodus 31:2–4 KJV Bold mine)

One work of the Holy Spirit that sometimes is overlooked is His endowment of wisdom and understanding in the working of earthly endeavors.

God tells Moses that He filled Bezaleel with the Spirit of God so that this man would have wisdom, understanding, knowledge in all things concerning workmanship (craftsmanship) and the materials and supplies needed within it.

THE PROMISE OF THE FATHER

The Holy Spirit was not only credited with taking part in Creation, calling men to repentance, and endowing men with spiritual revelation, but He also could grant men wisdom in things pertaining to life.

Bezaleel was not a good craftsman because it was his family trade, but the Holy Spirit gave him divine wisdom and knowledge as to how to build and how to use materials associated with building perfectly.

The Holy Spirit has always been an active force in the lives of God's people. He

THE PROMISE OF THE FATHER

was God's agent to reveal God's heart and empower God's servants.

The Promise of the Father

Israel was in trouble and God used Joel to reveal His displeasure. Yet, midway through his recorded prophecies, Joel makes an astonishing prediction of a future blessing,

> *And it shall come to pass afterward, that I will pour out my spirit upon all flesh; and your sons and your daughters shall prophesy, your old men shall dream dreams, your young men shall see visions: And*

THE PROMISE OF THE FATHER

also upon the servants and upon the handmaids in those days will I pour out my spirit. (Joel 2:28-29 KJV)

God promises that a time will come when He will give His Spirit in abundance to "all flesh." This prediction did not refer to a worldwide outpouring, but to an outpouring upon His people.

In the New Testament, this promise would extend to the Gentiles who would be grafted into relationship with Him by Christ. Remember, in the Old Testament times, the Spirit of God did not actively rest upon

THE PROMISE OF THE FATHER

ALL Israel, but usually upon those who were called to a particular ministry or service and the kings. It is understood that Joseph was a prophet and so the Spirit of God moved in His life.

God's Spirit rested upon all His prophets and prophetesses, and the priests, and the judges were acquainted with the Holy Spirit's activity, intimately. However, all the people did not experience the Holy Spirit in a direct, personal sense. They only experienced Him as He demonstrated His work in the servants of the Lord.

THE PROMISE OF THE FATHER

The Prophecy of Joel

God, in His wisdom and mercy, would no longer allow the Holy Spirit to be active in a "minority" of the people. It can be inferred that God made this promise to encourage the people that they would no longer be subject to disobedience and rebellion against Him without an internal help. Hence, the promise of the Spirit's outpouring would be God's response to the moral struggles of the nation.

Israel would not only reflect the holiness of God in religious rites, ceremonies, and the restrictions based

THE PROMISE OF THE FATHER

upon various aspects of their lives. They would reflect God's holiness by the indwelling and influence of His Holy Spirit.

Throughout the Old Testament writings, the descendants of Abraham knew about the Spirit of God and how He moved in the lives of certain individuals among the people. Therefore, the promise of an outpouring of the Holy Spirit, and its significance would be understood by those who heard Joel's prophecy.

The Foreshadowing of the Promise

Before examining the outpouring of

THE PROMISE OF THE FATHER

the Holy Spirit on Pentecost, an examination of Old Testament texts will reveal that Israel saw the outpouring of the Holy Spirit on numerous occasions, but not in the universal sense as promised in Joel.

Moses led Israel and was the chief prophetic voice. Miriam was a prophetess and it can be inferred that she exercised some influence for she led the women in praise after God's deliverance.

And Miriam the prophetess, the sister of Aaron, took a timbrel in her hand; and all the women went out after

THE PROMISE OF THE FATHER

her with timbrels and with dances. (Exodus 15:20 KJV)

While in the wilderness, Israel continued to complain and consistently burdened Moses for prophetic insight and leadership. The people has already been delivered from two major complaints, no water and no food. However, they became dissatisfied with the bread from heaven and grumbled because they wanted meat. Moses, being overwhelmed cried out to God for help.

Whence should I have flesh to give unto all this people? for they weep

THE PROMISE OF THE FATHER

unto me, saying, Give us flesh, that we may eat. I am not able to bear all this people alone, because it is too heavy for me. And if thou deal thus with me, kill me, I pray thee, out of hand, if I have found favour in thy sight; and let me not see my wretchedness. (Numbers 11:13-15 KJV)

Moses was frustrated. Before alleviating Moses' concern of how the meat would be provided for the nation, He first gives Moses a solution to him being the sole authoritative prophetic voice.

THE PROMISE OF THE FATHER

And the LORD said unto Moses, Gather unto me seventy men of the elders of Israel, whom thou knowest to be the elders of the people, and officers over them; and bring them unto the tabernacle of the congregation, that they may stand there with thee. And I will come down and talk with thee there: and I will take of the spirit which is upon thee, and will put it upon them; and they shall bear the burden of the people with thee, that thou bear it not thyself alone. (Numbers 11:16-17 KJV)

THE PROMISE OF THE FATHER

God promised Moses that He would take the spiritual prophetic endowment given to him by the Holy Spirit and will put it upon seventy men that Moses chose. When God fulfilled His promise, it mirrored the future events of Pentecost and beyond.

And Moses went out, and told the people the words of the LORD, and gathered the seventy men of the elders of the people and set them round about the tabernacle. And the LORD came down in a cloud, and spake unto him, and took of the spirit that was upon him, and gave it unto

THE PROMISE OF THE FATHER

the seventy elders: and it came to pass, that, when the spirit rested upon them, they prophesied, and did not cease. (Numbers 11:24-25 KJV)

When God placed the spirit (which was the Holy Spirit) upon the seventy elders, the experience was so forceful that they all began to prophesy spontaneously. It was so powerful that the men were unable to stop prophesying.

This is the first glimpse of what the outpouring would look like and what it would consist of. The men were taken out of themselves and could not prevent the

THE PROMISE OF THE FATHER

prophetic utterances that were coming from them.

God, in His wisdom, not only allowed the event to happen outside of the camp, but in the camp also because two of the chosen seventy were among the people when God placed the Spirit upon them.

But there remained two of the men in the camp, the name of the one was Eldad, and the name of the other Medad: and the spirit rested upon them; and they were of them that were written, but went not out unto the tabernacle: and they

THE PROMISE OF THE FATHER

prophesied in the camp. (Numbers 11:26 KJV)

Like the future Pentecost, God made His endowment of the Spirit a visible and notable feature. This occurred also so that the people would not just have to take a "blind faith" testimonial but could visibly see the Holy Spirit coming upon those chosen by Moses for prophetic leadership among the people.

When God placed His Spirit upon them, the men no longer had control over their faculties, but were moved by the Holy Spirit to prophesy in an uncontrollable and

THE PROMISE OF THE FATHER

ecstatic manner.

The next time a similar event occurred was at the calling of Saul to be Israel's first king. When he meets Samuel and is informed of his call to be king, Samuel prophesies to him of an extraordinary encounter with the Holy Spirit.

After that thou shalt come to the hill of God, where is the garrison of the Philistines: and it shall come to pass, when thou art come thither to the city, that thou shalt meet a company of prophets coming down from the high place with a psaltery, and a

THE PROMISE OF THE FATHER

tabret, and a pipe, and a harp, before them; and they shall prophesy: And the Spirit of the LORD will come upon thee, and thou shalt prophesy with them, and shalt be turned into another man. (I Samuel 10:5-6 KJV)

Saul was not known as a prophet or priest. However, to ensure his success as king, a promised encounter with the Holy Spirit accompanied with prophecy and praise (the musical instruments went before the prophets) is assured for him. Samuel's prophecy happened as predicted.

THE PROMISE OF THE FATHER

And when they came thither to the hill, behold, a company of prophets met him; and the Spirit of God came upon him, and he prophesied among them. And it came to pass, when all that knew him beforetime saw that, behold, he prophesied among the prophets, then the people said one to another, What is this that is come unto the son of Kish? Is Saul also among the prophets? (I Samuel 10:10-11 KJV)

Again, a spontaneous giving of the Spirit is given to Saul in a manner that was

THE PROMISE OF THE FATHER

forceful. He could not control what happened and his faculties became subject to the overwhelming influence of the Holy Spirit.

He, Saul, did something he never did before – he prophesied. A foreshadowing of the promise was given in another direct parallel. The Spirit's influence was powerful and induced spontaneous prophetic utterance.

When David fled from Saul and took refuge at Naioth, Saul sent messengers to take David by force. However, when messengers arrived there, on three

THE PROMISE OF THE FATHER

separate occasions, the Holy Spirit came upon them, overwhelmed them, and they prophesied.

> *And Saul sent messengers to take David: 0and when they saw the company of the prophets prophesying, and Samuel standing as appointed over them, the Spirit of God was upon the messengers of Saul, and they also told Saul, he sent other messengers, and they prophesied likewise. And Saul sent messengers again the third time, and they prophesied*

THE PROMISE OF THE FATHER

also. (I Samuel 19:20-21 KJV)

The messengers were interrupted from their task by the Holy Spirit overwhelming them and causing them to prophesy. When Saul finally came to inspect what happened, the same thing happened to him.

Then went he also to Ramah, and came to a great well that is in Sechu: and he asked and said, Where are Samuel and David? And one said, Behold, they be at Naioth in Ramah. And he went thither to Naioth in Ramah: and the Spirit of

THE PROMISE OF THE FATHER

God was upon him also, and he went on, and prophesied, until he came to Naioth in Ramah. And he stripped off his clothes also, and prophesied before Samuel in like manner, and lay down naked all that day and all that night. Wherefore they say, Is Saul also among the prophets? (I Samuel 19:22-24 KJV)

Again, an overwhelming experience of the Holy Spirit accompanied with prophecy is demonstrated. The Bible does not reveal the number of men in each group to apprehend David, but it had to be

THE PROMISE OF THE FATHER

enough each time to bind and restrain David to bring him back by force.

This account shows that on four distinct successive occasions, the Holy Spirit overpowered groups and inspired them to prophesy (though they were not prophets). From the above discussion, it can be concluded that the promise of the Father reveals that it will be characterized by certain features:

1. An overwhelming experience of the Holy Spirit
2. Physical reactions to Holy Spirit's presence

THE PROMISE OF THE FATHER

3. Prophetic Utterance

God's promise was fulfilled on the day of Pentecost. In the next chapter, the doctrine of the Baptism of the Holy Ghose will be discussed.

THE PROMISE OF THE FATHER

THE PROMISE OF THE FATHER

Notes:

THE PROMISE OF THE FATHER

-2-
The Baptism of the Holy Spirit

THE PROMISE OF THE FATHER

THE PROMISE OF THE FATHER

John the Baptist began his prophetic ministry while Judah was under Roman control. Their once proud nation was now one among many absorbed in the Roman Empire.

Those who were faithful to the Law of Moses yearned for deliverance from Rome oftentimes relying on prophecies given in the Old Testament about a coming Deliverer. Though Israel wanted God's deliverance, many have forsaken the Law and its precepts.

God sends John (known as the Baptist), to call the nation to repentance.

THE PROMISE OF THE FATHER

John understood that his ministry was the fulfillment of Isaiah's prophecy.

The voice of him that crieth in the wilderness, Prepare ye the way of the LORD, make straight in the desert a highway for our God. (Isaiah 40:3 KJV)

John came with a baptism of repentance. However, John understood that his physical baptism was the precursor to a coming baptism from the Lord.

I indeed baptize you with water unto repentance: but he that cometh after me is mightier than I, whose shoes I am not worthy to bear: he shall

THE PROMISE OF THE FATHER

baptize you with the Holy Ghost, and with fire: Whose fan is in his hand, and he will thoroughly purge his floor, and gather his wheat into the garner; but he will burn up the chaff with unquenchable fire. (Matthew 3:11-12 KJV)

Three Designations, One Event

John paralleled his physical baptism to the baptism of the Holy Spirit that was to come. The admonitions of John that the Lord would baptize followers with the Holy Spirit and fire is a direct reference to Joel's prophecy. Again, here is the first two verses

THE PROMISE OF THE FATHER

of the end time prophecy,

> *"And afterward, I will pour out my Spirit on all people. Your sons and daughters will prophesy, your old men will dream dreams, your young men will see visions. Even on my servants, both men and women, I will pour out my Spirit in those days. I will show wonders in the heavens and on the earth, blood and FIRE and billows of smoke. (Joel 2:28-30 NIV Emphasis mine)*

Along with the promise of the Holy Spirits outpouring, God details

THE PROMISE OF THE FATHER

events of the end time which will be characterized by blood, fire, and smoke. John's admonition to the people is an abbreviated expression of Joel's prophecy.

John was conveying that judgment will follow the outpouring of the Holy Spirit; hence, his listeners need to come to God with true repentance.

The Modern Doctrine

From the above, it is understood that the doctrine of the baptism of the Holy Spirit is not a modern invention or spiritual fantasy of Pentecostals, Charismatics, and

THE PROMISE OF THE FATHER

other Christian groups.

It is derived directly from the expressions of scripture. Jesus and John referred to the promise of the Father as being baptized with the Holy Spirit. Jesus interpreted it on this wise,

> *On one occasion, while he was eating with them, he gave them this command: "Do not leave Jerusalem, but wait for the gift my Father promised, which you have heard me speak about. ⁵For John baptized with water, but in a few days, you will be baptized with the Holy*

THE PROMISE OF THE FATHER

Spirit." **(Acts 1:4-5 KJV)**

Jesus equated the outpouring of the Holy Spirit, the Promise of the Father, and being baptized with the Holy Spirit as equivocal descriptions of what would happen on the Day of Pentecost. The Bible records then, three names for one event.

The Promise Fulfilled

On the day of Pentecost, as foretold by Jesus Christ, God fulfilled His promise and poured out His Spirit upon all gathered.

*And when the day of **Pentecost** was*

THE PROMISE OF THE FATHER

*fully **come**, they were all with one accord in one place. And suddenly there came a sound from heaven as of a rushing mighty wind, and it filled all the house where they were sitting. And there appeared unto them cloven tongues like as of fire, and it sat upon each of them. And they were all filled with the Holy Ghost, and began to speak with other tongues, as the Spirit gave them utterance. (Acts 2:1-4 KJV)*

The outpouring of the Spirit was exactly as instances portrayed in the Old Testament. In the first chapter, it was

THE PROMISE OF THE FATHER

stated that these three things characterized the previously stated manifestations of the Holy Spirit:

1) An overwhelming experience of the Holy Spirit

2) Physical reactions to Holy Spirit's presence

3) Prophetic utterances and praises

This event marked the birth of the New Testament Church. It signified a break from the Old Covenant practices for worship. In addition, revealed the nature of the New Testament Church which was to be guided by and characterized by an abiding

THE PROMISE OF THE FATHER

presence of the Holy Ghost.

The Doctrine of the Baptism of the Holy Ghost

To introduce the doctrine, it has to be considered that Jesus predicted that the apostles would be baptized with the Holy Spirit upon His departure.

Now, the Gospels record Jesus breathing on the apostles and commanding them to receive the Holy Spirit. Hence, we understand that the apostles, in particular, were already partakers of the Spirit's presence.

However, there was a baptism of the

THE PROMISE OF THE FATHER

Holy Spirit that was still forthcoming. This baptism would be characterized by a visible manifestation of power. It would enable the followers of Christ to be effective witnesses of His message and of His Resurrection.

The doctrine or teaching of the ***baptism of the Holy Ghost*** is not a Pentecostal invention. This doctrine states that after the regeneration of the Holy Spirit which baptizes members into the body of Christ, there is a subsequent baptism of the Holy Spirit available, which empowers believers to be effective witnesses of Christ's resurrection.

THE PROMISE OF THE FATHER

What is the scriptural basis for this assertion? The gospel of John records that after His resurrection, Jesus appeared to the disciples,

> *Then said Jesus to them again, Peace be unto you: as my Father hath sent me, even so send I you. And when he had said this, he breathed on them, and saith unto them, Receive ye the Holy Ghost: (John 20:21-22 Emphasis mine)*

These words mark a defining moment in the lives of His followers. They would no longer be disciples who sat for learning but

THE PROMISE OF THE FATHER

be sent ones to be demonstrators and propagators of the teachings they received. Jesus did not say to them that the reception of the Spirit was a future event, but a present reality.

This foreshadowed how individuals who would believe on Christ would be partakers of the Holy Spirit at the *new birth*. When Paul speaks of the believers being baptized into the Body of Christ, it is parallel to this experience of the disciples.

For by one Spirit are we all baptized into one body, whether we be Jews or Gentiles, whether we be bond or free;

THE PROMISE OF THE FATHER

and have been all made to drink into one Spirit. (I Corinthians 12:13 KJV)

From this we can conclude that the baptism of an individual by the Spirit into the Body of Christ is a ***separate*** phenomenon to what occurred on Pentecost. So then, where does the defined doctrine of the baptism of the Holy Spirit derives. It is first derived from Luke's account of Jesus' words of the forthcoming outpouring of the Spirit.

And, being assembled together with them, commanded them that they should not depart from Jerusalem,

THE PROMISE OF THE FATHER

but wait for the promise of the Father, which, saith he, ye have heard of me. For John truly baptized with water; but ye shall be baptized with the Holy Ghost not many days hence. (Acts 1:4-5 KJV)

For John baptized with water, but in a few days you will be baptized with the Holy Spirit. (Acts 1:8 KJV)

Jesus recalls that the promise of the Father was for individuals to be **baptized** by the Holy Ghost, analogous to water immersion. This is a significant observation because water baptism was an outward

THE PROMISE OF THE FATHER

sign of an inner transformation. Likewise, **the Spirit's baptism would come as a result of His inner dwelling of those who come to Christ.** This promise is not a necessity of salvation, but an outworking of salvation designed to empower Christians to testify of Christ's resurrection.

On the subject of baptism, it must be stressed that the New Testament makes mention of more than one baptism. The writer of Hebrews states,

> *Therefore leaving the principles of the doctrine of Christ, let us go on unto perfection; not laying again the*

THE PROMISE OF THE FATHER

*foundation of repentance from dead works, and of faith toward God, Of the doctrine of **baptisms**, and of laying on of hands, and of resurrection of the dead, and of eternal judgment. (Hebrews 6:1-2 KJV Emphasis mine)*

The writer of Hebrews states that there is a doctrine or teaching of *baptisms*, meaning, more than one. It can be concluded then that within the salvation experience that there is one baptism (done for salvation and entrance into the body of Christ). And there is another baptism performed by the Holy Spirit to empower

THE PROMISE OF THE FATHER

humankind for service in evangelism and edification of the local body. Paul elucidates this truth when he states that there are different operations of the Holy Spirit.

And there are diversities of operations, but it is the same God which worketh all in all. (I Corinthians 12:6KJV)

The Old Covenant revealed instances of "outpourings" of the Holy Spirit. These pointed to God's promise fulfilled on the Day of Pentecost with reverberating results in the life of Christian Church.

THE PROMISE OF THE FATHER

Notes:

THE PROMISE OF THE FATHER

THE PROMISE OF THE FATHER

-3-
Physical Manifestations & The Baptism of the Holy Spirit

THE PROMISE OF THE FATHER

THE PROMISE OF THE FATHER

Pentecostal and Charismatic Christians usually come under scrutiny and criticism because of the spiritual reactions of congregants.

In Christian services where people are seen crying, shouting, fainting, dancing, and the like, it is usually contributed to some kind of psychosis or religious fanaticism.

These critiques are flawed and contradict experiences of individuals who had experiences with the Holy Spirit under both Covenants.

It has been established, even in the

THE PROMISE OF THE FATHER

Old Testament, that encounters with the Holy Spirit engendered remarkable physical responses.

Hence, it is deemed necessary to demonstrate other Old Testament and New Testament experiences where physical manifestations accompanied encounters with the Holy Spirit. This should bring others to a clear perspective when judging Christian services where physical manifestations occur.

It has been established that the baptism of the Holy Spirit is compared to the practice of water baptism. Analogous to

THE PROMISE OF THE FATHER

water baptism, the believers in the upper room were *immersed* in His presence. This was in accordance with the words of John. How can this be asserted?

Those in the upper room were immersed in His presence. When those on the outside looked upon the disciples and heard their speech, they proposed that what they saw and heard was like intoxicated individuals.

For these are not drunken, as ye suppose, seeing it is but the third hour of the day. (Acts 2:15 KJV)

This statement could not be a direct

THE PROMISE OF THE FATHER

reaction to the speech of the apostles and the others because they were praising God in languages that could be understood by the gathering crowd. Drunk individuals' speech is commonly slurred and unintelligible. The apostles and those gathered spoke with *clarity* in other languages magnifying God.

> *And they were all amazed and marvelled, saying one to another, Behold, are not all these which speak Galilaeans? And how hear we every man in our own tongue, wherein we were born? Parthians, and Medes,*

THE PROMISE OF THE FATHER

*and Elamites, and the dwellers in Mesopotamia, and in Judaea, and Cappadocia, in Pontus, and Asia, Phrygia, and Pamphylia, in Egypt, and in the parts of Libya about Cyrene, and strangers of Rome, Jews and proselytes, Cretes and Arabians, we do hear them speak in **our tongues** the wonderful works of God. (Acts 2:7-11 KJV Emphasis mine)*

The charge of drunkenness can only be understood in the physical reactions of the individuals being immersed or **baptized** in the Spirit's presence.

THE PROMISE OF THE FATHER

Physical Responses in the Old Testament

In the Old Testament (as mentioned in chapter 1) there are accounts of physical reactions to the Holy Spirit's presence.

Daniel, the Priests, and Elijah

- Daniel fainted because the visions shown to him were overwhelming.

    And I Daniel fainted, and was sick certain days; afterward I rose up, and did the king's business; and I was astonished at the vision, but none understood it. (Daniel 8:27 KJV)

- At the dedication of the temple, the

priests could not stand and minister because of the presence of the Lord.

> *So that the priests could not stand to minister by reason of the cloud: for the glory of the LORD had filled the house of God. (2 Chronicles 5:14 KJV)*

- Elijah was energized by the Spirit and could outrun Ahab's chariot.

> *And the hand of the LORD was on Elijah; and he girded up his loins, and ran before Ahab to the entrance of Jezreel." (I Kings 18:46 KJV)*

THE PROMISE OF THE FATHER

Balaam, Samson, and Saul

- When the Holy Spirit came upon Balaam, he fell into a trance.

    And Balaam lifted up his eyes, and he saw Israel abiding in his tents according to their tribes; and the spirit of God came upon him. And he took up his parable, and said, Balaam the son of Beor hath said, and the man whose eyes are open hath said: He hath said, which heard the words of God, which saw the vision of the Almighty, falling into a TRANCE, but having his eyes open:

THE PROMISE OF THE FATHER

(Numbers 24:2-4 KJV Capitalization mine)

Peter and Paul had similar experiences recorded in the New Testament.

- Peter fell into a trance and the Lord revealed to him His acceptance of the Gentiles.

    And he (Peter) became very hungry and would have eaten: but while they made ready, he fell into a trance. (Acts 10:10 KJV Parenthesis mine)

- Paul fell into a trance while he was in prayer.

THE PROMISE OF THE FATHER

And it came to pass, that, when I (Paul) was come again to Jerusalem, even while I prayed in the temple, I was in a trance. (Acts 22:17 KJV)

Trances are usually followed by visions. This was a promised outcome of the Spirit's outpouring.

- The Holy Spirit came upon Samson to energize him to perform great acts of strength.

    And the Spirit of the LORD came mightily upon him, and he rent him as he would have rent a kid, and he had nothing in his hand: but he told

THE PROMISE OF THE FATHER

not his father or his mother what he had done. (Judges 14:6 KJV)

- The Holy Spirit came upon Saul in a powerful fashion when Israel was threatened by Nahash. In the Hebrew, the term translated "come upon" is in Hebrew צָלַח H6743 tsalach. It literally means to rush. This denoted a swift and definite physical experience of the Spirit's \presence.

    And, behold, Saul came after the herd out of the field; and Saul said, What aileth the people that they weep? And they told him the tidings of the men

THE PROMISE OF THE FATHER

of Jabesh. And the Spirit of God came upon Saul when he heard those tidings, and his anger was kindled greatly. (I Samuel 11:5-6 KJV)

Looking at the events following, we discover that the force of the Spirit upon him caused him to be energized for battle, in the same manner that it caused him to prophesy after Saul reveals to him that he would be king (see I Samuel 19:22-24 KJV).

- When Saul pursued David, upon he and his men's arrival at Ramah, the Holy Spirit came upon him and he prophesied. The intensity of the

THE PROMISE OF THE FATHER

experience caused Saul to lose his outer

garments.

And he stripped off his clothes also, and prophesied before Samuel in like manner, and lay down naked all that day and all that night. Wherefore they say, Is Saul also among the prophets?" (I Samuel 19:24 KJV)

Jeremiah, the Seventy Elders, Abraham, Isaiah, & Elisha

- Jeremiah said that the word of God was in Him so powerfully that it felt like fire shut up in his bones. It provoked him

THE PROMISE OF THE FATHER

physically so that he would respond to the Lord's direction to return to his prophetic ministry.

Then I said, I will not make mention of him, nor speak any more in his name. But his word was in mine heart as a burning fire shut up in my bones, and I was weary with forbearing, and I could not stay. (Jeremiah 20:9 KJV)

- In Numbers 11, when God took of the Spirit upon Moses and placed upon the seventy chosen men, it states that they prophesied continuously. They were

THE PROMISE OF THE FATHER

under the Spirit's influence in such a way that it could not be resisted.

> *And the LORD came down in a cloud, and spake unto him, and took of the spirit that was upon him, and gave it unto the seventy elders: and it came to pass, that, when the spirit rested upon them, they prophesied, and did not cease.* (Numbers 11:25 KJV)

- Abraham fell into a trance when God spoke to him in Genesis 15 after Abraham's request for a guarantee on God's promise to him.

THE PROMISE OF THE FATHER

And about sunset a trance fell upon Abram, and lo! a great gloomy terror falls upon him. Genesis 15:12 BST)

- Isaiah stated that the Lord spoke to him with a strong hand.

    For the LORD spake thus to me with a strong hand, and instructed me that I should not walk in the way of this people. (Isaiah 8:11 KJV)

    This signifies the experience was physically intense.

- Playing music sometimes is a vehicle for the Holy Spirit moving upon God's

THE PROMISE OF THE FATHER

people. Elisha requested a minstrel to come and play, and then the Spirit of God moved upon him to prophesy.

*But now bring me **a** minstrel. And it came to pass, when the **minstrel** played, that the hand of the LORD came upon him. (2 Kings 3:15 KJV)*

Physical Manifestations in the New Testament

Physical responses to the Holy Spirit's power occurred repeatedly in the Old Testament and continued in New Testament times. Hence, the assumption of drunkenness was the result of the Holy

THE PROMISE OF THE FATHER

Spirit's overwhelming (baptizing) power. Physical responses to the Holy Spirit's moving continued to be a common phenomenon.

Even after the events of Pentecost, the baptism of the Holy Spirit was seen as an overwhelming experience, accompanied by prophesying and praising God. At Cornelius' house, in particular, we see it as an overpowering occurrence.

Those gathered were sitting in anticipation of Peter's full message of salvation. However, the Holy Spirit interrupted the setting and came upon

THE PROMISE OF THE FATHER

everyone, who immediately began to speak in tongues.

While Peter yet spake these words, the Holy Ghost fell on all them which heard the word. And they of the circumcision which believed were astonished, as many as came with Peter, because that on the Gentiles also was poured out the gift of the Holy Ghost. For they heard them speak with tongues, and magnify God... (Acts 10:44-46a KJV)

It was an immediate sign of God's reception of the Gentiles and a further

THE PROMISE OF THE FATHER

continuation of Jesus' promise of His followers speaking with new tongues.

And these signs shall follow them that believe; In my name shall they cast out devils; they shall speak with new tongues; (Mark 16:17 KJV)

The experience of those at Cornelius' house demonstrates another dimension of the baptism of the Holy Spirit into the Body of Christ for salvation and the baptism of the Holy Spirit for power: They can occur simultaneously. This was first demonstrated at Pentecost.

THE PROMISE OF THE FATHER

The eleven disciples were the only ones who experienced Jesus' breath upon them for reception of the Holy Spirit. The other disciples and women in the upper room were neve said to have had this experience. However, when the Holy Spirit came upon them, they were received as members of the Body of Christ and endowed with a visible manifestation of His power, concurrently.

Years later, when Paul presented the full gospel message to John's disciples, they had this simultaneous experience as well.

THE PROMISE OF THE FATHER

When Paul placed his hands on them, the Holy Spirit came on them, and they spoke in tongues and prophesied. (Acts 19:8 KJV)

John's disciples had not yet believed on Christ and were still waiting on the baptism that John prophesied would come. To verify John's prophecy and the truth of Christ as the Son of God, they believed and received the Holy Spirit.

These accounts were given so that those who believed on Christ would not be surprised by this phenomenon and trust the experience. When looking at

THE PROMISE OF THE FATHER

Christianity's history, it is peppered with God granting this experience to Christ's followers. They have been referred to as reformations, outpourings of the Spirit, revivals, and renewals.

When these events occurred, speaking in tongues was oftentimes a by-product. These things are of record. They were not isolated events, but even occurred in churches whose teaching and doctrine rejected modern-day manifestations of the Holy Spirit. However, God has never been bound by man's teaching.

Those who are acquainted with

THE PROMISE OF THE FATHER

Church history know that tongues and miraculous manifestations of the Spirit occurred long after the apostles and the first century disciples' death.

In referring to modern times, events like the Azusa street revival of the early 20th Century and the latter Charismatic renewal which occurred, all came about as the Holy Spirit invaded "traditional" churches and people spoke in tongues and prophesied.

Time would fail to speak of similar revivals which occurred in European nations such as England, Ireland, France, and Scotland. Every time where many were

THE PROMISE OF THE FATHER

converted to Christ, these revivals were characterized by a tangible presence of the Spirit, speaking in tongues, and accompanied with physical reactions being the feature of most of them.

THE PROMISE OF THE FATHER

-4-

The Gift of Tongues

THE PROMISE OF THE FATHER

THE PROMISE OF THE FATHER

Though many have purported imaginary and hypothetical times where the Holy Spirit would no longer give certain gifts of the Spirit, they are all conjugations of the mind.

One thing must be stated: the gift of tongues and other gifts of the Holy Spirit did not cease after the deaths of the 1st century Christians.

The Biblical record, itself, reveals that as new communities of Christians were established, the gifts of the Holy Spirit, including tongues, continued.

To separate the gifts and to assert

THE PROMISE OF THE FATHER

that some stopped while others continued is patently unwarranted. Paul speaks of the gift of tongues in a common fashion along with teaching and pastoral ministries in the Church. One can trust that the Holy Spirit did not divide His work because of time.

The completed New Testament did not replace the need for the gift of tongues and prophecy, and other gifts to operate in the Church. The Old Testament Jews had the Law, yet God still used prophets among the people. The prophets were not needed to replace the Law but be vessels for God's

THE PROMISE OF THE FATHER

immediate interaction among His chosen people. The prophets ministered, at times, to help individuals in their lives and to fulfill particular callings of God.

Likewise, the operation of spiritual gifts in the Church were never designed to replace the scriptures. They were given to edify members in the body of Christ. God, in the New Testament, still called individuals as prophets and certain people were known to have the prophetic gift.

Now, concerning tongues, there is much unfounded and unnecessary theories and teachings surrounding this gift. In this

THE PROMISE OF THE FATHER

chapter, clear definitions and explications of the manifestation of tongues will be provided.

What is the Gift of Tongues?

The gift of tongues is a gift of the Holy Spirit whereby prophetic utterances, prayers, and praises are expressed in the Body of Christ. The gift of tongues found its first expression on the Day of Pentecost. However, it was not the sole operation and manifestation of this gift. On the day of Pentecost, the people gathered did speak in tongues in the known languages of the people gathered.

THE PROMISE OF THE FATHER

Now, it is understood that God did this to demonstrate to all of the differing nationalities His power. However, from the letters, the tongues that manifested in the Christian assemblies did not all manifest as known languages. A fallacy that is promoted is that if someone is speaking in tongues, it has to be in a known language.

God empowered those on the Day of Pentecost to speak in known tongues as a sign to all the people who were gathered. It was intended to help them believe on Jesus Christ. However, in the churches, Paul asserted that people could speak in

THE PROMISE OF THE FATHER

tongues and no one will know what is being said.

Hence, the need for the spiritual gift of the interpretation of tongues is given by the Spirit. If all tongues spoken were in a known language, then the gift of interpretation would be unnecessary. The church would only need a translator.

When in operation, this gift allows the individual to speak in a language that is unknown to the speaker. This is where the power of God is displayed. In the Old Testament when the Holy Ghost came upon Saul and the men that he sent, they

THE PROMISE OF THE FATHER

prophesied without control, as did the seventy men whom God placed Moses' spirit upon. The gift of tongues seizes the individual's faculties and allows then to speak, sometimes seemingly uncontrolled, in differing languages.

> *For he that speaketh in an unknown tongue speaketh not unto men, but unto God: for no man understandeth him; howbeit in the spirit he speaketh mysteries. But he that prophesieth speaketh unto men to edification, and exhortation, and comfort. He that speaketh in an unknown tongue*

THE PROMISE OF THE FATHER

edifieth himself; but he that prophesieth edifieth the church. I would that ye all spake with tongues, but rather that ye prophesied: for greater is he that prophesieth than he that speaketh with tongues, except he interpret, that the church may receive edifying. (I Corinthians 14:2-5 KJV)

The gift of tongues manifests for three different purposes: *prayer, prophecy, and praise.* When considering the New Testament epistles, this will become clear.

THE PROMISE OF THE FATHER

Prayer

Tongues can be a feature of a Christian's prayer time for personal edification and comfort. The Holy Spirit helps the believer to pray the will of God. Paul states that the Spirit of God knows the mind of God. Therefore, the Holy Spirit, at times, will invade the believer's prayer time. This may occur at times in the public, congregational setting during corporate prayer.

*For if I **pray** in an unknown tongue, my spirit prayeth, but my understanding is unfruitful. What is it*

THE PROMISE OF THE FATHER

then? I will pray with the spirit, and I will pray with the understanding also: I will sing with the spirit, and I will sing with the understanding also. (I Corinthians 14:14-15 KJV)

Tongues are manifested in prayer to also bring edification into the believer's life. Paul states that the believer who speaks in an unknown tongue will be edified; that is, built up in the faith. Tongues during personal prayer times may not always be accompanied with interpretation because the Holy Spirit is making intercession on the believer's behalf.

THE PROMISE OF THE FATHER

And he that searcheth the hearts knoweth what is the mind of the Spirit, because he maketh intercession for the saints according to the will of God. (Romans 8:27 KJV)

If the gift of tongues is manifested during corporate prayer, then someone with the gift of interpretation should be there to know how the Spirit has aided through the interpretation.

Prophecy

Remember, tongues in the public assembly are not to be forbidden. However, those who use this gift should use

THE PROMISE OF THE FATHER

discretion and use this gift without interrupting the service or drawing undue attention to themselves. To use tongues as a way to prove one's spirituality or garner attention is misuse and abuse. This was what was happening in the Corinthian church. Individuals would use tongues to show their spirituality and no one was edified.

> *If there is **no interpreter**, the speaker should keep quiet in the church and speak to himself and to God. (I Corinthians 14:28 KJV Emphasis mine)*

THE PROMISE OF THE FATHER

Paul states that when someone speaks in tongues, it should be in a responsible and non-invasive way in the assembly. To keep quiet means to be controlled; however, Paul did admonish the individual to SPEAK to himself and God.

Tongues are never to be forbidden in the church, but those who will draw attention to themselves must be prepared to interpret the tongues or know of someone in the assembly who has the gift of interpretation, so that the church is edified by this gift.

THE PROMISE OF THE FATHER

When the gift of tongues is accompanied by the gift of interpretation, it stands in the same class as prophecy. If someone is speaking in tongues in an open and obtrusive way, and interpretation is not there, Paul states that this is treating others in the assembly as if they were unbelievers. Paul refers to the Old Testament to clarify this point.

In the law it is written, With men of other tongues and other lips will I speak unto this people; and yet for all that will they not hear me, saith the Lord. Wherefore tongues are for a

THE PROMISE OF THE FATHER

sign, not to them that believe, but to them that believe not: but prophesying serveth not for them that believe not, but for them which believe. (I Corinthians 14:21-22 KJV)

In the Old Testament, when God wanted to judge unbelieving Israel, He would use foreigners who spoke in languages that the Israelites did not understand to defeat them in battle. Hence, the unknown languages that the Israelites heard was an open sign of God's displeasure with their forsaking of the Law.

THE PROMISE OF THE FATHER

To speak in unknown tongues without interpretation is tantamount to treating Christians in the assembly as unbelievers. Therefore, Paul states that tongues without interpretation would represent God's displeasure in the assembly.

However, if they are interpreted (equal with prophecy), they are treating those present as believers. Speaking over an assembly in tongues, without interpretation is a bad prophetic sign, for it is a spiritual demonstration of God's displeasure rather than His approval.

However, tongues that are spoken in

THE PROMISE OF THE FATHER

a forceful and upright manner accompanied by interpretation edifies the whole assembly and will speak to the congregation to edify, exhort, and comfort in the same manner as prophecy.

> *But he that prophesies speaks to men to edification, and exhortation, and comfort. (I Corinthians 14:3 KJV)*

Remember, again, when Paul speaks of tongues verses prophecy he states,

> *I would that ye all spake with tongues, but rather that ye prophesied: for greater is he that prophesieth than he that speaketh with tongues, except he*

THE PROMISE OF THE FATHER

interpret, that the church may receive edifying. (I Corinthians 14:3 KJV)

In his discourse, Paul wished that everyone spoke in tongues. This shows how important he viewed tongues and their operation in the lives of believers. However, in the assembly, he deemed its operation more viable if it is accompanied with the gift of interpretation.

Praise

When recounting the biblical passages of tongues. A feature of the recorded events was that the individuals also praised God. On the day of Pentecost,

THE PROMISE OF THE FATHER

it is first seen.

> *Cretes and Arabians, we do hear them speak in our tongues the wonderful works of God. (Acts 2:11 KJV)*

The people heard those in the upper room recounting (praising) the wonderful works of God. This continued when the Spirit fell in the house of Cornelius.

> *For they heard them speak with tongues and magnify God. (Acts 10:KJV)*

Presently, in times of intense praise and worship services, individuals will begin to speak in tongues. This phenomenon is

THE PROMISE OF THE FATHER

seen regularly and is fairly common among those who do speak with tongues. These tongues, if interpreted, will be revealed to be praises magnifying the Lord. Remember, the gift of tongues may also manifest in prophetic praise songs and singing.

I will sing with the spirit, and I will sing with the understanding also. (I Corinthians 14:15b KJV)

Believers who do not speak with tongues must guard against unnecessary restrictions to their manifestation in the church. Remember the words of Paul,

THE PROMISE OF THE FATHER

Wherefore, brethren, covet to prophesy, and forbid not to speak with tongues. Let all things be done decently and in order. (I Corinthians 14:39-40 KJV)

Paul's admonition was to not deny the operation of tongues but ensure that they are exercised in a proper and well-behaved manner.

*Else when thou shalt bless with the spirit, how shall he that occupieth the room of the unlearned say Amen at thy **giving of thanks**, seeing he understandeth not what thou*

THE PROMISE OF THE FATHER

sayest? (I Corinthians 14:16 KJV Bold mine)

Edification through tongues and only be achieved though the accompanying gift of the interpretation of tongues, as tongues are exercised properly.

Interpretation of Tongues

The companion to the gift of tongues is the gift of interpretation of tongues. This gift is necessary to bring understanding to utterances that are given through the gift of tongues. We have aforementioned that the gift of tongues manifests in three ways: prayer, prophecy, and praise.

THE PROMISE OF THE FATHER

Therefore, when an utterance in tongues is given, the interpretation will fall into one of these categories. Many have tried to confine the interpretation of tongues to only expressing a prophetic word.

However, the interpretation of tongues is needed to bring understanding to expressions of prayer and praise given in tongues. In this way, the whole church is edified, strengthened, and encouraged.

Wherefore let him that speaketh in an unknown tongue pray that he may interpret. For if I pray in an unknown

THE PROMISE OF THE FATHER

tongue, my spirit prayeth, but my understanding is unfruitful. What is it then? I will pray with the spirit, and I will pray with the understanding also: I will sing with the spirit, and I will sing with the understanding also. Else, when thou shalt bless with the spirit, how shall he that occupieth the room of the unlearned say Amen at thy giving of thanks, seeing he understandeth not what thou sayest? For thou verily givest thanks well, but the other is not edified. (I Corinthians 14:13-17 KJV)

THE PROMISE OF THE FATHER

Paul made it clear that if someone speaks in tongues, they should ask God for the gift of interpretation. So, whether in prayer, praise, or singing, it is imperative they have an understanding.

This is so the church may receive edification. The use of this gift is rarely seen in the Church today, while the gift of tongues is seen almost regularly. This was never the plan or intent of God. The challenge for today is to seek after God that this gift would become as important as the gift of tongues.

THE PROMISE OF THE FATHER

THE PROMISE OF THE FATHER

-5-

Questions & Answers

THE PROMISE OF THE FATHER

THE PROMISE OF THE FATHER

In this chapter, common questions concerning tongues and the baptism of the Holy Spirit will be addressed.

Question 1 - Is speaking in tongues a requirement of salvation?

NO. The manifestation of speaking in tongues is given to those who have *already* believed. Speaking in tongues can only occur in those who have already believed and have the Holy Spirit's presence. Though it did happen simultaneously to those present in the house of Cornelius as Peter preached.

Remember, on the day of Pentecost,

THE PROMISE OF THE FATHER

there was a mixed group. There were the disciples who had already been recipients of the Holy Spirit (signified by Jesus breathing upon them). And there were the other followers of Christ who were praying in expectation of experiencing the outpouring of the Holy Spirit.

When the Holy Ghost came, the eleven disciples of Christ were baptized by the Spirit ***only*** because the Holy Spirit was already present with them. However, the others that were gathered received the Holy Spirit (because they had believed on Christ) ***and then*** experienced His baptism

THE PROMISE OF THE FATHER

(at the same time), signified by their speaking in tongues along with the eleven disciples.

Question 2 – Should I ask for the gift of tongues?

Yes. Paul did instruct the Corinthians to covet or desire the best gifts. Just remember, if you ask for the gift of tongues also ask God for the gift of interpretation, if He wills it to be so.

> *But covet earnestly the best gifts: and yet shew I unto you a more excellent way.(I Corinthians 12:31 KJV*

Paul also said it was his personal

THE PROMISE OF THE FATHER

desire that all in the church spoke with tongues. His personal desire is not a spiritual mandate; however, it demonstrates the possible value of the gift of tongues in an individual's life.

Question 3 – Can children speak in tongues?

Yes. Any one of understanding and faith, regardless of age can be saved, filled with the Spirit, and speak with other tongues through the Spirit's unction.

Question 4 – Do all tongues must be in a known earthly language?

No. On the day of Pentecost, the

tongues manifested in known languages. However, in Paul's discourse to the Corinthians, he referred to tongues that were unknown.

> *Wherefore let him that speaketh in an **unknown** tongue pray that he may interpret. (I Corinthians 14:13 KJV Bold mine)*

Hence, the need for the gift of interpretation of tongues was needed.

Question 5 - What does *interpretation* of tongues mean?

Tongues are to be *interpreted* and not necessarily translated. When tongues are

THE PROMISE OF THE FATHER

interpreted, the **meaning** and **message** of the Lord is explained. Except the tongues manifest in a known language, a spiritually induced interpretation of message will come to being understanding and edify the church.

On the day of Pentecost, no one with the gift of interpretation was needed because the people heard tongues that were spoken in known languages. In the assembly, Paul advocated for someone with the gift of interpretation to be involved when *unknown* tongues were spoken.

THE PROMISE OF THE FATHER

Question 6 – Does one have to speak in tongues in order to have the gift of interpretation of tongues?

No. The gift of the interpretation of tongues is not dependent upon possessing the gift of tongues. They are two distinct gifts that operate in distinctive fashions.

This is why Paul stressed the necessity of someone who can interpret tongues, to bring balance to someone who speaks in an unknown tongue. A person can interpret tongues without ever having spoken in tongues personally.

THE PROMISE OF THE FATHER

Question 7 - Are tongues that are sang are only for praising the Lord?

No. Remember, a significant portion of the scriptures were psalms and sang in temple worship. Tongues that are sung, when interpreted, may carry prophetic exhortations to the congregation. Remember, God told Israel that He would joy over them with singing.

The LORD thy God in the midst of thee is mighty; he will save, he will rejoice over thee with joy; he will rest in his love, he will joy over thee with singing. (Zephaniah 3:17 KJV)

THE PROMISE OF THE FATHER

Question 8 – Do tongues that occur in private require interpretation?

Sometimes. If the individual has the gift of interpretation of tongues, they may exercise this gift if this is how God chooses to speak to them even in private. However, interpretation is not always necessary in one's private devotions. An individual should not be afraid to interpret tongues that are given to them in private.

Question 9 – Is speaking in tongues the sole evidence of being filled with the Spirit?

No. Many believers are filled with the

THE PROMISE OF THE FATHER

Holy Spirt without speaking in tongues. Remember, Paul asked the rhetorical question of whether everyone spoke with tongues. The answer was NO. Remember, the true sign of being filled with the Holy Spirit is in a godly lifestyle.

Question 10 – Can the gift of tongues be imparted through the laying on of hands?

Yes. However, this can only occur through the leading of the Holy Spirit. Again, no gift can be imparted except there is an *unction* of the Holy Spirit to do so. Though God may allow His Spirit to be

THE PROMISE OF THE FATHER

manifested through the laying on of hands, one must remember that the ultimate dispersal of the gift is from God and not the "act of laying on of hands" in itself alone.

Question 11 – Does everyone that speaks in tongues have the gift of tongues?

No. Everyone that speaks in tongues does not have the gift of tongues. Paul describes the gift as diverse kinds of tongues. The Greek word for "kinds" mean that they will speak in different sorts of languages in tongues.

To another the working of miracles; to *another prophecy; to*

THE PROMISE OF THE FATHER

another discerning of spirits; to another DIVERS kinds of tongues; to another the interpretation of tongues (I Corinthians 12:10 KJV Emphasis Mine)

The person who has the gift of tongues will speak in tongues with a greater dimension and in various manifestations which will require the accompanying gift of interpretation.

Hence, individuals may speak in an unknown tongue for personal use and edification and not necessarily for the edification of the entire body.

THE PROMISE OF THE FATHER

When someone has the gift of tongues, the "kinds" of tongues that they will speak under inspiration will be in different manifestation as the occasion demands. Their tongues will even sound different from one setting to the next unlike others who speak in the "same" tongue under inspiration.

THE PROMISE OF THE FATHER

THE PROMISE OF THE FATHER

Notes:

THE PROMISE OF THE FATHER

www.ingramcontent.com/pod-product-compliance
Lightning Source LLC
Chambersburg PA
CBHW050342010526
44119CB00049B/654